LEAF IS ALL

Leaf is All

Drew Dillhunt

SHABDA PRESS
DUARTE, CALIFORNIA

Leaf is All © 2022 by Drew Dillhunt

Printed in the United States of America.

First edition, Bear Star Press, 2015

Shabda press
Duarte, CA 91010
www.shabdapress.com
Email: shabdapress@yahoo.com

Cover by Jason Puccinelli
Book design by Beth Spencer
Author photograph by Jim McCabe

ISBN: 978-1-7377113-5-3
Library of Congress Control Number: 2022942920

ACKNOWLEDGMENTS

Grateful acknowledgment is made to the editors of the following publications and anthologies in which earlier versions of some of the poems first appeared:

Eclectica: "Numerology"
Mudlark: "Cover Letter"; "3,068,518";
    "Plastic #1 [2-Liter Bottle]," "Plastic #2 [Hula Hoops]
    "Plastic #3 [LP]," "Plastic #4 [Tupperware],"
    "Plastic #5 [Thermals]," "Plastic #6 [Styrofoam],"
    "Plastic #7 [Nylon]," "Plastic #7 [Teflon]"
the needle can: *An Anthology of Poetry*: "Exemplar," "The concept of remedy
    is tenuous at best," "Leaf is All"
Newborn: *A Book of Verse*: "Parallax"
The Pitkin Review: "Plastic #2 [High Density Polyethylene]"
VOLT: *from* "Herselves"

To those without whom this book would not exist, adequate thanks are not possible:

Frank X Walker, Elena Georgiou, Juliana Spahr, and Paisley Rekdal, whose words, inquiries, and vision are constant guides; Kary Wayson, whose inspired vision helped my manuscript find its current form;

CX Dillhunt, who raised me with poetry; Kathy Koegel, who led me toward the unwavering curiosity of mindfulness; and Kelley, an exacting proofreader, for all of it.

Thanks also to Ellen Welcker, Emily Johnston, Jeff Encke, and Teresa Mei Chuc for lending their eyes and insight to these poems; to Jason Puccinelli for his artistic vision and shared passion for Goethe; and to Chris Shuck, who graciously lent his statistical skills to the task of generating the daily world population numbers (highly precise but of questionable accuracy) that pepper these poems.

Contents

/•/

Dear Gordon,

Let me begin by saying I am frightened and uncertain. Frightened in the way I was when your mother and I moved out of our one-bedroom apartment and bought this house for $209,900 two days after 9/11. A fear that finally passed the day I repaired the lock on the front storm door by replacing the metal circlip with an E-clip I found in a plastic drawer at Lowe's Hardware on Rainier. The only tools I needed were two screwdrivers (one Phillips and one slotted). I feel obligated to include here a narrative that explains how I am already so in love with you and how I'm anxiously awaiting your arrival. The truth is I'd be happy with a few more weeks of things the way they are.

When you talk to me later, my perspective on this point will have changed—not because I'm a liar, but because the truth has been transformed. I'll tell you how those were the happiest times of our lives (which they were/n't) and how desperately we miss them (which we do/n't). You may even have begun to develop the erroneous impression that we knew where we were going and what we were doing (which we did/n't). This is what I want to tell you. Love is full of regret; hope is plagued with doubt.

It has been a strange spring filled with hail and cold snaps. I continue to turn on the fan each night as a sleeping aid. On nights when your mother asks for additional blankets, I simply put it in the corner and face it towards the wall. I suspect you'll like the white noise machine we're planning to buy for you.

This morning your mother confided that the room spins each time she turns over in bed to ease the pressure on her hips. I suggested that it might be the result of blood being redirected in large quantities. What frightens her most is the unpredictability of her dizziness—it never happens when she stands up.

If this is to be a time capsule, it seems important to include more than just words, so I'm also sending an unopened copy of Billy Strayhorn's posthumous *Lush Life* along with the new Andrew Bird album— both of which I have been listening to incessantly over the last nine months.

Already,

Papa

dd
Under separate cover:
1. *Armchair Apocrypha*
2. *Lush Life*

/ · /

a.   *Hypothesis: all is leaf.*
          This simplicity makes possible the greatest diversity.
                              — Goethe

b.   *I just want to say one word to you—just one word—plastics.*
          There is a great future in plastics. Think about it.
          Will you think about it?
                              — The Graduate, 1968

c.   *What do you want—a cliff over a city?*
          A foreland, sloped to the sea and overgrown with roses?
                              — Muriel Rukeyser

d.   *You spoke*
          for me of my cell,
          I'll not work its silence and peace again—
                              — Louis Zukofsky

e.   *Dearest, I cannot loiter here*
          in lather like a polar bear.
                              — Robert Lowell

f.   *John Hopkin Hospital and all other places,*
               that has my mother cells, don't give her
          Nothing.
                              — Deborah Lacks

g.   *Is "I" even me or am "I" a gearshift to get from one*
          sentence to the next? Should I say we?
                              — Claudia Rankine

Leaf is All

It's a cliché, your breathing.
back | open

who's the jumping jack
ever invented?

I ask the wind, as it struggles
to stay within, a thread

to mesmerize
this notion of togetherness

nodules, we grow
impatient splitting component parts

and the city's grid
full of nodules too

: [a cotyledon] unto us all, heartily
gentrifying the divide

growth and motion
In intimacy they stand, the tender pairs

time-lapsed, the tendrils
          forth | closed

Flinging the chain unto the end of time—

Plastic #1 [2-Liter Bottle]

I built a simple terrarium
from a 2-liter soda bottle.
When the sun rises, clouds form
and rain falls down the rounded plastic walls.

I want to squeeze my body through this threaded opening
twist the bottle cap back on from behind
and stand beneath the sympathetic bows of miniature mimosa forests—
gaze out at the world through the cloudy plastic
picture windows of my new enclosure.

At the zoo down the street, there are more than a few tears
when a Mylar balloon filled with helium
is accidentally released from the hand of a child
looking intently at the lions.
We watch it float away and wonder
Where will it come down?

We release a space station
coated in Dacron and filled with astronauts
wearing polyester fleece to keep their feet warm.

In a small container that pulls down from the wall,
the ceiling, or the floor, a mimosa plant is being grown
to study the effects of shyness on microgravity.

Water empties from vacuoles
as blood drains from a face—
leaves lying down
in carefully organized rows
raise questions about the true extent
of human influence.

From the collapsible aluminum lawn chair in the backyard
I can just make out two bright little specks in the sky:

Numerology

one

It began with coffee pots
lids, baskets, and percolators—
large pots and a factory promotion came later

despite fraternal warnings about fast work
and piece counts.

I didn't move to Chilton
so much as wait to move away.
My work ethic: an expression
of my need to pay

the rent on a downtown house, where
I could walk to the hospital.

On my third application I finally lied.
Any mention of seasonal work was left out
so the floor boss could reassure the union
he wasn't hiring part-timers.

Like everyone in town
he recognized the scars on my face,
wanted me to find work.

He had just been waiting
you suggested years later

for me to read between the lines.

Notes on "Numerology"

Equivocation is ubiquitous (and indispensable). The only thing we need you to recognize is yourself in our confusion.

To meet as far this morning
From the world as agreeing
With it, you and I
Are suddenly what the trees try

To tell us we are:

The concept of remedy is tenuous at best

when your mother sits with you
in the kitchen chair, your arms around her neck. There,
I reach over her shoulder, coax down your lower lid—
run a bead of erythromycin along the redness.
Excess is caught up in your lashes
as you work your swollen eyes—
a scrim of clear gel that blurs everything:

the tenuousness of conception is a remedy at last.

1

3,068,518

APPARATUS FOR MOLDING HOLLOW PLASTIC PRODUCTS

5

Kelley A. Couvillion, Seattle, and Andrew K. Dillhunt,
Seattle, WA., assignors, by mesne assignments to
Mold-A-Rama, Inc., Los Angeles, Calif.,
a corporation of California.
Original application Sept. 20, 1957, Ser. No. 2,919,828.   10
Divided and this application Sept. 3, 2008, Ser. No.
6,809,547.

8 Claims. (Cl. 18-26)

This invention relates to an apparatus for quickly   15
and accurately molding a quantity of hollow plastic
products such as plastic figures, toys, and the like.[1,2]

---

[1] When I meditate, I imagine I have no internal organs. I am alternately hollow and entirely solid. I am the waxy-white, molded polar bear I bought from the automated vending machine at the Brookfield Zoo with a handful of quarters, gentle and smooth. A polyethylene hologram of perfection. K has no such luxury. She has two of everything. Two sets of kidneys. Two sets of ears. Two sets of eyes. Two noses, two livers, two hearts.

[2] The plastic aerator (disguised as a deep-sea diver) goes up and down in the fish tank.
I ponder the circumpolarity of my life, then yours.

Herselves

for Henrietta Lacks

Let me be the first to say
I am not a research scientist

but as I listen
to the State of the Union

while bathing my son
it occurs:

I am human too
the blood on this vaccine

mine: the way only another's
presence in the room

contains

/•/

Insurgent tissues

are part of the state
until they go

renegade, and then?
And then

there's the resonance
of a daughter

opening a freezer door

/•/

A horse, a woman, and a man

My father, who is neither
a horse nor a woman,
wishes he were instead
a white mare.

Middle-class iconoclast
overflows ping-pong ball
Bozo Buckets at six a.m.
Channel 9 WGN Chicago
endless piles of toys.

       How high is have?

My father is a white mare
which must make me
an alabaster pony.
We are both of us women
both of us black as oil
both as brown as loam.

       How slow is surreal?

My mother, who is neither
a horse nor a man,
is quite aware of reality.

Privilege is a giraffe.

These long arms reach for succulent green.

Leaf is All

A feather is a weighty construct
once fossilized
impervious to the clock radio

Of flowers, spread athwart the garden, Aye,

how to explain a pear is not a pearl—
memories as vigilant as trying

to back up the drive.
Standing on the wall, you're the height
of the city when we embrace

the real numbers disappear *Papa,*
I don't believe in _____. What do you think?

The traffic is distraught. We *are* traffic

practically, about the moment
on the count of three I put the ducklings in my pocket

Took now this form, now that, in swift succession!

Leaf is All

It's the sentiment of the raspberries
she cuts from the terrace:

why don't we want / dandelions in our yard?

the mock orange we once boxed
to near nothingness

now curvilinear tips in triple-space
a pair of Steller's jays in the pear apple

the root-stalks merely an impression
of the limbs, I insist

the precincts of the city do the same
To limb, itself repeating,

Numerology

two

The bridal shower would have been
April 18, 1970.

We drove the "ORD" that night
from Milwaukee towards Green Bay
(always on the lookout for an "F"
to replace the one missing from the trunk).

You in the front seat,
my sister, also Kathy
in the back with Biblio
a friend's dog she'd volunteered
to watch for the weekend.

The police refused to believe.
The insurance company was disappointed.
It'd been a simple cocktail
of long hours in study halls
followed by late dinner.

And how peculiar the down payment
on our first house
the result
of your agency litigating mine.

You arrived in a hearse

because for an ambulance
Chilton was too small.

Notes on "Numerology"

I would know that thought if I thought it again, is a thought that cannot effectively be expressed, embedded as it is in the internal logic of the system.

Suffice it to say: "I can't remember."

Plastic #2 [Hula Hoops]

Relax. Listen to your eyes as they embark on separate journeys.

HDPE is the polymer plastic used in the production of milk jugs, detergent bottles
and Hula Hoops.

Focus on nothing and you'll find
HOPE, instead.

This walleyed position is known, when it occurs medically, as diverging strabismus.
The trick is to relinquish conscious control. In fact, this technique can also be used to
discover the hidden sailboat, or space shuttle, in those frustrating computer-generated
pictures, which at first glance appear to be nothing more
than gaudy, flowered wallpaper.

Once you've managed to achieve this for yourself, hold it.
Extend your duration with each attempt.
Build your retinal stamina.

Soon, you'll have the happy experience of filling reusable canvas bags with HOPE
instead of plastic, each time you visit your local grocer.

With practice you may even manage to spin
HOPE around your waist
hips perfectly synchronized with the undulating wobble
of the earth's precession, the pulse of a Hawaiian pop song.

A drawstring, a polar bear,
an approximation

The cotton of my pajama bottoms, where
the drawstring has begun to tear

holds the faded pattern of polar
bears. the blue polyester cuffs of my fleece

gather here
in my hands. I want things

to go on like this
I want to go on forever like this

the Siamese cat whose eyes cross
looking too long in sunlight

tucked between us morning's traffic
pulses the wet pavement and airplanes

head south over the backyard.
I want things to go on forever like this.

I'm 32. my father is 59.
I want to stop counting

how old he'll be when I'm 50.
the paint on the windows is

caked with exhaust.
3 months after you're born I'll be 33.

I want to go on like this.
the desk lamp's halo—not yet

disrupted by morning's sun.
I want to go on forever like this

the idea of a baby
(an approximation

of a polar bear)
growing in your stomach.

I want to want like this:

Let the sentence decompose.
this is where the carbon goes

There are **two blue lines**
on the horizon this morning

crowded together
in the bathroom

we see violet streaks
the aurora borealis

peeking through the window
of our home pregnancy test.

Herselves

There, there, rational thought

the time-lapse of the infinitesimal
contains a moment (s

in a roller drum)
where we find the crux

to feign sleep: now there
's a sign of prescience

where's the medium
to nurture faith?

must we plunge a needle in
-to the heart of a bantam

or will it suffice to lay hands?
I'll break stride

to name the immortal
at the top of a Ferris wheel (a stolen image

a marker of time) a nucleotide sequence (I
don't want to tell it for you

can I borrow your mirror
to acknowledge it all (would be preposterous

not to (o (predictable?
it's not all provenance

here we are (tucked in the shirt of his pocket,
there, there) nutrients and body warmth

unlike Carrel's chicken heart
for real in the quietude

of what will

/•/

'

[4] Our complementary surfaces
have been in alignment for going on

nine months now. It's a continual process
of recalibration, of sliding back and forth.

A machine having a plurality of complementary mold sections which sequentially engage and disengage each other, a hollow plastic product being automatically formed during the cycle of operation when the mold sections are in mutual engagement. [3]

20

25

We claim:

1. In an apparatus for molding hollow products of a plastic capable of melting upon heating and of passing into a hardened state upon cooling, a pair of mold sections having opposing surfaces provided with complementary recesses. [4,5]

30

[5] The question is: when
will we disengage the machinery?
Which direction will we move
relative to one another

                    and what does it mean
to be a father in the 21st century?

Leaf is All

In the case of the body, I open

to the curve of the pear apple's trunk
to the swell of her thigh on summer's couch.

This must be mindfulness, to examine
the propelled body

in some way nearer to the self
redefining what it means to be vegetal.

I'm lost in the representation
chalked on the wall of the café.

I have the four pennies, I say to the cashier
not knowing what to expect in return.

The leaf unfurls as a series
of near-colored petals.

There are nodes after all, we say half-
astonished in quiet corners.

Expansion & contraction.
Expansion   & contraction.

None but must marvel as the blossom stirs

Leaf is All

Identify the transitional forms
from brownstone to residential ring

The plant-child, like unto the human kind—

remember: all is leaf
from calyx   to corolla to   stamen

where a dormer thrusts
its doubled flower through the pitch

of the roof, caressing
the nectary's surplus value

the way you rescue the bamboo clippings
from the neighbors' yard waste

lodge them in an empty flower bed
Think how our tender sentiments, unfolding

Plastic #3 [Vinyl]

The Beatles sound best on vinyl. The fidelity of the compact disc ignores historical
context, whitewashes the curvature of sound waves. Harmonies accommodate the random
hopping of the needle, overtones of dust.   Perfection is
an accumulation of tiny flaws. White noise is different, each time you listen.

The expanse of the suburb is caked with it. Grooves are etched into plastic in an attempt
to create the illusion of wood. Vinyl siding is weatherproof, scratch-proof,
and never need be repainted.   It is also a lie.   In an age so obsessed with information,
doesn't this feel like a terrible waste of space?

Housing developments are a parade of Edison phonograph cylinders
waiting to have grooves cut. Houses talk, when voice is given.   An oversized stylus
(easily integrated into the design of future ladders) is all that's needed to listen. Climbing
to the roof to clean the gutters no longer need be a chore. On your way up, listen

to the tribulations of past generations. Discover the previous occupants of your dwelling.
How Jenny broke her leg in the backyard jumping from the swing set. How Carl fell in love
with the neighbor boy's golden curls. How yesterday all their troubles seemed so far away.
We could take this a step further.   Magnetize strips of vinyl weatherproofing

before they leave the factory. Attach a letter to each one containing an unbelievable offer
that can't be refused. Turn neighborhoods into piles of credit cards with 18% APR
and no late fees until next year. Think of the combined maximums on all those rows
of magnetic strips.   A cul-de-sac of debt.

Numerology

three

In my own hospital room
after the accident
I wondered about Biblio (he was, after all
the only reason I could ever remember the word library
in Spanish) about my sister Kathy
about you
sleeping in the front seat.

Sometimes, when I'm shaving, a piece of glass
works its way out.

I cradle it in my hand.

Sometimes, you don't wake up
until you've hit a tree.

Notes on "Numerology"

The act of trimming Ben-Day dots for a storyboard—think Lichtenstein's *Drowning Girl*—entails forgiveness, where forgiveness is the grief of one generation co-opted as the creation myth of the next.

Recently he explained, "I feel responsible for everything. I don't want to hit a tree again and sometimes I feel like I'm going through a forest."

[6] Community is the allegory through which the ideas for the moving parts of machines are birthed.

[8] Physical = $\sin(2\pi t/23)$, Emotional = $\sin(2\pi t/28)$, Intellectual = $\sin(2\pi t/33)$, where t = the number of days from birth.

[7] Diagnostic tools need not accurately portray reality in order to have meaningful effects on the way we make sense of the world. Such is the poetry of type I statistical error.

[9] We never imagined we'd discover backward masking in the rhythmic sounds of the breast pump.

2. A frame providing a horizontal platform,[6] a pair of mold sections movably mounted upon said platform for horizontal movement in opposite directions,[7] and means for cyclically moving each of said mold sections between a first position wherein said opposing surfaces are in contiguous relation and a second position wherein said surfaces are spaced apart.[8, 9]

35

40

A saltlick, a surgeon, and this

My love, who is neither
a saltlick nor a surgeon,
wishes she believed
her cowlick came from the kiss of a cow.

We're a different tangle—
clues on the body never enough.

Father told her
tales:
the green beans always
from the farmer's farm.

       Have we shrugged the apricots?

There's an indentation in my chest
where she'd press the scalpel—if
she didn't love me. Between
my ribs, love
is a skein of skin.

       Have we peeled the precious?

Her sister's gone.
The motorcycle: still here,
the blue plush bunny left packed
in an emptying house.

Have we stanched the stem?

A drawer is organized in many ways
only opened in one.
We breathe together.

I rub your neck in concentric
circles; I try
chocolate, crushed ice.

It's astonishing
how hard a body can push
without progress.

The bathtub is confined
in space, in time.

My little boy suggests we'll both fit.
We both fit.

The water looks as deep as it is.
We pour it over and over ourselves.

We both know we won't fit tomorrow.
We hardly fit here now.

He puts a toy in the bowl for me to pour.
I pour it with the water on my hair.

He pours it with the water.
The water has gone from clear to gray.

We're always older after than before.
We giggle as the soap scuttles the side.

We watch the gray gutter the drain.
I'm the foolish one

wanting this graywater
to saturate the garden.

Our effluence is recycled
like—

Herselves

to know
our lacks

to surface
a space

where

caress = reticulum

w_here

analogy = eros(ion)

w__here

paradox = verb

w___here

the cell(f) is at war

w____here

edge = tourniquet

w_____here

metadata ∴ doubt

w_____here

decomposition $\subset$ embrace

w_____here

cell = body

w_____here

secession = faith

Henrietta,
is this your gift

: a place where
our cell(ve)s

become one

/•/

Henrietta,
your cells [*the weeds*

of cell culture]
are prayers

of intercession,
moments of formidable

forgiveness, sites
of enzymatic silence

strange, the way we
[*real humans*]

translate the language
of thanks

/•/

Earth nite
threaten I

inert heat
retain the

the retina.
Irate then

attire hen
titan (here)

at neither
at therin

tat inhere.
A tether in

a / ether tin
a heir nett:

heart-tine.

44

Leaf is All

I don't see: your hand cradling his
Above the slender framework of its leaves

the fingernails clip on the sound of distance
my finger snaps no photo.

The city is full of discreteness
of right angles, of mail-in ballots.

The airport is liminal
A germ begins to burgeon here and there,

the calyx and corolla, two
sides of the same topology.

There are specifics that fall from the sky—

like the pigeon that crapped on the web of my hand
the pinecone that plummeted against my brow.

Yesterday, I told you how I'd saved it
as if we never have the kind of details we need.

Leaf is All

As violins play the sonata,
G draws his hands from his lips
one over the other:

I'm pulling air from my mouth.

The sun rises over the overpass.
We call it a leaf because it expands

the kitchen table, this morning so plain

To see, each leaf elaborates the last—

the canopy slips the foreground
against the middle-

ground and background

in stride's inspection
branches unmuddle

To limb, itself repeating,

this form and that
name themselves again

Numerology

four

The only one belted in was me—

and still, without a shoulder strap
to avoid collision with the steering wheel.
In the break room, a few play cards.
There isn't much need for talk
among tired men. I eat bologna sandwiches
and drink Mt. Dew to keep myself alert.

This work is my meditation—

I hear only the thump-pop
of the aluminum press, the whir of belts
and the quick sound of the wrist guard's snap
returning my hands
to safety at my sides.

This machine is my rosary—

I see that spot, and the tree
somewhere between here
and Hilbert on Highway 57,
in the pressed reflective bottom
of each piece of cookware.

Notes on "Numerology"

Today I saw the truth of perspective: twin lines diverging in all directions from the point origin of me. A generation is a footnote appended to a footnote, which is why the act of having a child engenders the unmistakable sensation of immortality

                              and what

        does an academic

                                    forest look like

note to self: are you here

Plastic #4 [Tupperware]

"Secrets will stay fresh for weeks,"
said the hostess, as she burped the avocado bowl
cradled in her hands.

The ladies opened and closed the ladies
developed a keen sense of the ease
with which things can be stored inside—

liberation never as simple as bending
in the right direction at the right time.

She was more than willing to embrace the facade
of high heels and hose to ease
executive minds. She was

a prophet peddling enlightenment
and everything
was about to come apart at the seams.

Eventually, she would slip and fall
on the carpet of her living room floor
out of reach of the volume knob and further from the phone
forced to listen
to the *Moonlight Sonata* on repeat
while she waited for the paramedics.

The orthopedic surgeon replaced one side of her hip
with a pliant piece of milky-white plastic
designed to cradle her calcified femur.

The doctor chose the anterior approach and sealed her back up
with a straight line of stitches.

As a boy, he grew up surrounded by women. His mother was a woman and she had five sisters, so all of his aunts were women as well. His maternal grandfather had died when he was two, which meant that his grandmother, his mother's mother, was perched upon a matriarchal layer cake. His cousins, his aunt's daughters, were little women, the neighbor children—all five of them— were girls, and even his father (who had grown up surrounded by sisters) believed he was a woman. This is how it is, he thought to himself.

Parallax

We've been listening to the stars
with radio telescopes,
watching the sound of your heartbeat,
the sonority of the valves
as they open and close.

They might as well have been light years—
five spiraling metacarpal galaxies
expanding exponentially
in grainy black and white
closing back in again on themselves.

I don't mean to confuse color with sound
the electromagnetic with the mechanical—
this art of making
image from echo
vibration from light.

The measurement was twelve weeks
from crown to rump.
According to the technician
we were lucky to have heard them at all
from this early angle

fingers tend to look like paddles
just as distant stars sometimes appear

depending on your vantage
to occupy a single point in space.

We may have mastered the algorithms
for looking in, but what I want to know is this:
what constellations are projected tonight
on the dark lining of your planetarium?

Metropolis

Me, oil ports.
Me, oil sport.

Me, pilots, or
me-pistol, or

me spoilt, or
me, soil sport

Re: limo spot
me: lip roost.

Me: lips' root.
Lip, torso: me.

Riots pol, me.
Riots, lop me

re: mi sol pot.
Me, riot slop.

Re: imp stool
re-tips loom.

Re: I lop Ms. To.
Lo, I re-pot Ms.

Re-, tip sol, *om.*
Re: Spilt Moo,

I re-lost mop.
Me, lisp root.

Me, slip root.

Me: lips Oort.

Me, silt poor
me, list poor.

Me, poor stil
me: lit spoor.

Poor elm, sit.

Poor elm, its
melt is poor.

Lest, mi poor

me-slit, poor.

Plot is me, or
me: roils pot.

I storm pole
petrol, mi so.

Petrol, I oms.
Petrol *is* om.

Slope mi rot.
Lore I stomp.

Lore mi pots
lore tis mop.

Lore, its mop.
Lore: it mops.

Role I stomp.
Role: "-ism" pot.

Loser imp to
lose mi post.

Lose prim to
sole I tromp.

To prim sole:

lept I rooms
pelts I moor.

[moor = lept]
[lept = room]

Lest me poor,
pelt Sir Omo.

[room = pelt]
[pore = molt]

Lest I promo
Miss Poor, tel.

lets rip *Moo.*

Lo, mores tip—

more lips to
more slip to

more "I" plots.

Smote or Lip?
Poem or List?

Lo, poem stir.

Metros I lop
some lip rot.

Me: trip solo,
REM-pilot.

REM lip-soot
perm oils to

sperm oil (to)

Romeo split
Romeo spilt.

Milepost, or
or, milestop

or, lei-stomp
smile-opt, or

lei mops rot

Lei, Ms. Troop?
Lei, Mr. Stoop?

Peril Tom, so
Peril Ms. Too.

Pile Mr. Soot
Pile Ms. Root
Pile Mrs., too.

Loiter, Ms. Po.
Toiler: Ms. Po.

Oriel, Ms. Opt?

Plies Tom, or
Plies Mr. Too.

Relit mop, so
lies *om*-port:

Tile Ms. Oops.
Tile Ms. Poor.

Sol tempi: or.

Morel, I spot

Morel tip so
morsel, I opt

Molter, pi so
Motel psi, or

Elms, Trio Op!
Elms, Tiro Op!
Elms, Riot Op!

Tore so limp—
Elms, rip too.

Elms, poor it.
Elms: pi root.

Elm posit, or
Elm: pi roost.

Elm *is* troop

Elm, its poor
Elm: sip root.

El, poor Smit.
El import, so

El, mi troops.
El, mop torso.

El, prim soot!
El, prism too

tire, sol mop.

El pits room.
El tips room.

El, room's tip.

El trim, *oops*,
El "-ism" troop.

El, sip motor.
El psi: *motor*.

Mole, sip rot.
Elm, sip Oort.

More "I" plots

mole tips, or
mole: Sir Top.

El rips moot.

Móle, Sir Opt?

Prelim soot
politor *oms*:

simpler too
simple root.

More pistol,
more spoilt:

REM topsoil.

Islet promo
implores to

impel roost
impel torso
pile motors.

Toilers mop
moper's toil.

Peril moots
moot pliers

prelims too.

Isomer plot:
Ripest loom

tremolo psi.

Tropes moil
tempos roil:

more pilots.

Herselves

I swear,

there's connectivity
in the prefix: *cyto-*

from κύτος
for jar

/•/

the implied privacy of a medical record

here it is floating—

the history / of night
doctors

as inseparable from the culture

of cells
as the intervening sky: astounding

/•/

a protein lodged in the bilayer;

a pair of fluorescent Xs
emblazoned on the night sky;

the inside of the body
studded with pearls;

a cleanroom
a shrine

/•/

below said platform and comprising a valve casing having a bore therethrough, a movable valve member within said bore, and means for sequentially moving said member between a first position wherein source of molten plastic communicates with flow passage and a second position wherein source of compressed air communicates with said passage.[11]

5

---

[10] Kelley's water broke on her first good push. The doctor shielded herself with a clear plastic apron and ducked out of the way like a bullfighter.

[11] This morning I felt the polar bear kick. Or was it a hiccup?

When I'm with you it becomes manifest that *change is love.*

3. The structure of claim 2 in which means are provided for pushing plastic products formed by said mold sections out of the path of the same while said sections are spaced from each other.[10]

4. A valve assembly for controlling the flow of molten plastic and compressed air to said mold sections, said assembly disposed

45

Leaf is All

Eyes flicker,
curl into a corner.
An apology contains
a whole truth

relevant only to remorse.

The seed is contraction
and the fruit expansion
all is leaf—

Foreshadowed pattern, folded in the shell,

a placard on the bus, entitled thus:

we've been here before.

Leaf is All

The first leaves are paired, and later
where they alternate

Here are the berries, the edible plants,
my love, have you tried the salal?

In the same light, that lovers may together

The apples espaliered on
the property's edge

where the skyline bar graphs and
the letterscape implies a plane with

a rhombus
inscribed on a blackboard

Of shape and structure shown in succulent surface—

Must we always enter
through the bathroom window

now that we've lost our keys
Juggling requires

more balls than hands

I still have all the reel-to-reel recordings
he made of us in our basement.

How many hours did he spend crawling around on the floor
with a microphone, before I had anything to say?

I am listening to you listening to yourself
through the scratchy static of turning magnetic tape

hoping for some instructions (c. 1977)
that might explain how to handle the world.

At the very least, it would be nice to learn how
to correctly thread a blank reel so

the contents transfer
without twisting during playback.

Herselves

[intercession]

Scientise nor
resection sin

insistence, or
consent is ire

consent rise "I"
consent I sire:

icier sonnets,
coteries / inns.

/•/

icon sire tens
icon ire nests

icon rinse set
icon seers tin

icon rises ten
icon sister en

icon sentries
icon stir seen

icon: en rests I
icon, it enters

/•/

tininess core
riot in scenes

ironies' scent
is tensin core

cistern noise
intones crise

cistern is eon
censer I into

censer, is it on?

/•/

tocsin rise en
tocsin siener

notice sirens
notice resins

notice rinses
notes crise in

note, nice sirs
note, nicer sis:

onset cries, "in!"

/•/

enter icon sis
enter scions, I

recite in sons
incise re: tons

cosset inner I
stereo [*sic*] inn

tonne cries, "is!"

/•/

ice risen tons
ice rents ions

ice store inns
ice en sis, torn

ice sterns, "I, no."

/•/

irenic onsets
irenic stenos

irenic stones:
Icon in Esters / Esters in Coin

scions enter I
& rest in cosine

sonnet cries, "I!"

/•/

scene in riots
scene in trios

scene in torsi
scene in intro

scene: I sir, ton
scene: I in sort

scene: I is torn

/•/

(*iris, not scene*)

/•/

I centers ions
I cession rent

I cisterns eon
I scions enter

inner cites so
inner [*sic*] toes

inner cote: sis
inner sect, so I

risen notices
cites risen on

risen ((tics)) eon

Plastic #5 [Thermals]

Diaphanous fibers
birthed from melted slurries / of 2-liter
soda bottle tops. Metal dies extrude
bolts of milky-white
fabric / cut to fit
our silhouettes
keep us warm
if we'll insulate
/ in return.

> *Machine Wash Cold*
> *Line Dry*
> *Do Not Iron*

I fill the pockets of my parka
with plastic bottle tops
to protect myself / from frostbite.

Articles dyed blue / dyed red
create an allusion to softness
/ and warmth.

> when did you realize / your long johns
> could melt

Microscopic barbs / stick to my lifelines
the catching feeling of sandpaper, the
expression of fingernails
on chalkboards. Unpleasantness
of microfiber dust rags / now we're comparing
plastics to plastics.

10   5. The structure of claim 4 in which said means comprises an air-operated piston connected to said movable valve member for moving said member between first and second positions.[12]

15

---

[12] There's something about self-organizing phenomena that's convincing. Of something. There's this transition from the technical, to the techno-emotional, to the melodramatic (and then back again).

The melodrama at the living room bar develops as the in-sound of the phonograph becomes the out-sound of the soundtrack: Mrs. Robinson offers Benjamin a drink.

A teacher, a nurse, a ventriloquist

My mother, who is neither
a hat nor a ventriloquist,
wishes she were instead
her mother's hatpin.

Who quotes the quilt?

Efficient in the sandbox
saves the college fund,
a tenderness of common sense
dreaming all its own.

The tonic on the piano rings
through the Christmas carol,
head on her lap
on the way to the hockey game.

Who flattens the fabric?

Practiced about the moment, and practical
beyond protective hands.
The can-opened lid cuts the flesh
in the down-pressed garbage; open
to examine the fat cells of the wrist
sweep these in too.

Who sensibly senses the slip?

There are times
when Mars was misidentified as an airplane.
There are times when
we talked to the passenger in the next seat.

My father is becoming my mother
—a thing of beauty.

We never break our hearts, except
to miss and miss like this.

Numerology

five

[Room 117]

We rescheduled our wedding plans
enlisted hospital staff as attendants.

Gladys Dingledine
your first roommate
your maid of honor
checked in for lung cancer

technically, of course, she was a matron
but we never met her husband.

Skip Schmedelkauffer
the physical therapist
whose mother was your nurse
my best man.

The entire hospital staff as witnesses,
lurking happily in your doorway.

Vivian, the young nurse—
I can't remember her last name—
she inspired you to go back to school—

she baked our cake and found a knife.
Don't look so worried, she said,
it didn't come from surgery.

Notes on "Numerology"

It's easy to tell how much someone loves you from the way they prepare the mail. What I really want to sightread are the rest of the labels on your manila folders. What I want to hear is the green writing of your felt-tipped marker. The Greenbelt Network. The Green. Belt. Network. What is the Greenbelt Network?

Notes on "Notes on 'Numerology'"

Make certain to practice the following folding techniques: *the no-pins method, the flying angel wing, and the twist.*

somewhere, I've read

the closest a man can get
                                                    to giving birth

is a good car accident.

Leaf is All

In last light's babble of

who are we to stay:
I'm me, I'm me, I'm me

Has the lake lost its depth, divined
or another pencil mark on the door frame?

Here, water!
between our twinning
shells.

If goggles make you float
shadows grow from / tendrils, the

streetlights in more directions—this one
shrinking that one
growing

The rich profusion thee confounds, my love.

The goings of
your breath, it means
to be confused

See—this C
of shadows more interesting
than clouds or ocean of

my love, my love, where
is the first node, the coffee shop,
the quintet?

Hollyhock, foxglove, I've learned some names
you love, the chickens, you love

the notes
can I pet the white one?

you name the hedge—we walk past
red cedar, red cedar, red cedar, red

Leaf is All

The pedant examines
the infinite details of the incomplete

sentence, they clear as he zooms
the pixelated space-time of

the hayfield—
these technicalities, correctly

combined, unearth justified
disequilibrium:

Don't confuse me with the facts,

L intones
from the back of the town car

The nub of tranquil life, kept safe and dry,

Numerology

six

some days it feels as though
we are collecting sevens:

17
the number of roommates
with whom you shared
room number 117

57
the number printed on the highway marker
next to the tree

7-21-70
the date we were married
(21 is a seven
in triplicate)

17
the date in April
when I fell asleep last—

don't think for a moment
that a seminary boy like me hasn't noticed seven
is the number of the Extreme Unction

Plastic #6 [Styrofoam]

The hotcakes are tucked into
the polystyrene blankets.

The serrated edge of
the knife skips the surface.

The fork leaves
the four puncture wounds

to fill themselves
with syrup.

The baby carrots wrapped in pale
yellow paper, and emblazoned

with the scarlet letter *M*—
they taste better to preschoolers.

I save the cardboard container
from the cookie-cutter hashbrowns, because

it reminds me of a little red speedboat.

How your ears dip below the surface   how your eyes widen   how you recline with your feet in the air   how the instructor plunges you under   how your legs and arms flap   how your eyes are pressed shut   as you burst back out   how your head sways from side to side how your arms string around my neck   **how you cling to the island of papa**   how we pour a cup of water over your head   in the kitchen sink   to wash away the soap   how your muscles twitch   with memory   how pleased I am to know   you're here again already.

This all occurred as an autonomic function of our bodies. Not only were we not in control of these developments, we weren't even really aware of them. My genotype called out to your genotype in the dark and heard an answer—even if it *was* only an echo.

15   6.   In an apparatus for molding hollow products of a plastic capable of melting upon heating and passing into a hardened state upon cooling, a valve member having an intermediate portion of reduced transverse

20   dimensions providing an annular space within said bore adapted for alignment with said flow passage of said casing.[13]

  7.   The structure of claim 6 in which said casing is provided with a chamber therein,

25   said casing also providing an inlet and outlet to chamber for the circulation of a heat-containing fluid therethrough.[14]

  8.   The structure of claim 6 in which piston means are provided for sequentially

30   moving said valve member between said first and said second position within said bore.[15]

[14] I have an irrational fear of randomly generated numbers. I'm unable to resist the urge to dislodge obvious patterns, the clear evidence of tampering. Random never looks random enough.

[15] Breathe

Herselves

Here [is where]

our telomeres shrink
the explosion divides
my cell(ve)s

see it: a blood test: we

demarcate an organ system
explicate the singular
insist the cognates are false

a body is a body

I remind my selves
not to speak
the voice of others'

mitochondria

imply a shared cell(f)
blurred in culture / where

there can be no such motion
as speciation.

/•/

O Henrietta,

the way you've taken
this poem

infiltrates / my sense
of the body

where selves rendezvous, Henrietta,

does appropriation ever become
/ an exercise in tenderness

/•/

Notes on [a] Form [Letter]

CCA CARLE CLINIC ASSOCIATION

602 WEST UNIVERSITY AVENUE · URBANA, ILLINOIS 61801· TELEPHONE (217) 337-3113

March 24, 19█

IN FURTHER CORRESPONDENCE
REFER TO CLINIC NUMBER

new[1]

Mr. ███ Dillhunt,
1203 Briarcliff
Urbana, Illinois 61801

Dear Mr. Dillhunt,

Our records show that we reserved a 15 minute pediatric appointment for you with Dr. Wolf on March 24, 19█ at 9:10 which you did not keep.[2] When an appointment is made, the time is reserved on the doctor's schedule.[3] Failure to keep the appointment or to cancel two days in advance delays other patients from obtaining medical treatment and wastes the doctor's time.[4]

We realize that in an emergency situation you may not be able to give us two days advance notice of a cancellation.[5] We will appreciate your letting us know as far in advance as possible that you will not be able to keep your appointment.[6, 7] If this should happen again, please call us.[8] *We may be able to schedule someone else in your place.*[9]

Yours truly,

J.D. Carr
Credit Manager

---

[1] This is a letter about falling in love.

[2] About the careful time in between, and the careless time that follows.

[3] About the gravity of politics, the gravity of cells.

[4] The human body is best understood through the metaphor of machines. I dropped my notebook in a dream and the pages scattered everywhere; I chased after each of them like a lover after a train car.

[5] Lover number one puts hand on lover number two's waist. Lover number three unbuttons shirt, sits on bed, pulls back covers. Lover number four closes bedroom door.

[6] Lovers number six and seven hold each other close in evening air, take in city vista from park bench. Lover number five cradles head in hands, wonders when lover number eight will take notice, be sent off on tour of duty, or return from corner grocery.

[7] …while opening anatomical gift with scalpel, lover number 3,097,366 glimpses the underlying logic of it all.[a]

[8] When an accountant writes a letter to an infant, it's a mechanical response, and yet a tender one.

[9] This letter could have been written to any one of us, at any time; this letter has been written by all of us, at one time or another.[b]

[a] The heart of poetry is a hollow man / a heteronym, a forensic test, & casino chip†

[b] The present invention contemplates an artificial heart that can be mounted inside the body of a patient as a replacement or substitute for a removed heart.†

† Winchell, Paul or Gizzi, Peter. "Artificial Heart" or *Artificial Heart*. U.S. Patent 3,097,366. 16 July 1963 or Providence, RI: Burning Deck, 1998.

Transmission

I've tried on nothingness like a verb.
I rewired an old lamp to fit the decor.

My car resists being shifted—

something about
a shredded servo, a variation

on the word transmission:
the trunk of a car is a mystical place.

Shall we investigate?
I have a map of the city's intersections

composed entirely of questions about the moon.
How it knows where your house is.

And where do the exes enter
your diagram of the city: a blow job

on the interstate, a string bikini glimpsed
through the sliding glass of the cosmos

the way he walked in on us falling into one
another one

Leaf is All

There's ecstasy in beginnings.
Tuck the security blanket,
the crumpled Kleenex beneath your nose.

I'd put you in one pocket
and G in the other, offers my father
at the terminal, his roller bag

before the security checkpoint.
That's because you're his little boy
offers my little boy.

The word "clutch" hovers,
a cotyledon: a clutch of eggs
a clutch of hand-holds

to make the to-do list.
The clutch finds the carpet
as we ro-cham-beau the night sky

Joining another cycle to the last,

Leaf is All

Queen Anne's lace dappled with
its red floret—
the wild carrot
on the prairie, an import.

The wasp won't see
                                    a pinprick, it sees
the nectar of the moment

don't you say it
a vegetable is not a metaphor for
a glacier is not a metaphor for

We tread the gully to stand
in a bevy of outsized grasses, we touch

where the silk is softer
than what it is.

at length attaining preordaining fulfillment

The father is not the metaphor
for the son, the father
is not the metaphor

and the lights are flashing
and we already know it
what to call them:

Notes on "Notes on 'Notes on "Numerology"'"

As we mold our forebears into our own likenesses, it becomes more and more difficult to say for certain.

Exemplar

We arrive on the Jumbotron like the
happenstance of a dugout

the way *umpire* sounds a touch
like *Empire.*

Entropy begins at the ocean of desire.
We have some friends, who have some friends

and tickets for the usher at the stairs.
From here, just east of home plate

I can see
all there is to love
about baseball.

This is life! I shout

to the little boy bobbing
in his father's arms
in time
to the seventh-inning stretch.

We were propaganda for the moment,
and the National Pastime of closing our eyes.

I'm hardly even chagrined
now
as I tell you

we reveled in it.

Plastic #7 [Teflon]

I put a hex on myself
just before I enriched our kitchen
with space-age polymers.

I was investigating freezers
when one hundred pounds of TFE gas
spontaneously polymerized.

I was four of a mind,
trapped and frozen, shoulder to shoulder
inside steel cylinders.

I rested on a bed of dry ice
braced myself for the rupture
of impending disaster.

/•/

I was disappointing and waxy—
a white solid soon to be revealed
as the world's slipperiest material.

I didn't worry
until I was told I would have to give up
my metal spatula for wooden and plastic.

At that moment, I began
to obsessively watch the soft surface
of cross-hatched frying pans
for any indication
of flaking residue.

/•/

It's the Cold War
I shield my eyes with frying pans
I solve my problems with separation

and correct the market slump
by counting down from 2% to skim.

I shoot television spots
as the president; I
[presciently] sport a milk mustache
to mollify our worry
over the indictment
of milk fat as an agent
of heart disease,
Soviet tests over the Pacific

and accumulations
of strontium-90
in our children's milk supply.

/•/

Nuclear physicists at Oak Ridge
struggling with the corrosive properties
of enriched uranium hexafluoride gas
were the first handymen
to plumb their pipes with Teflon.

Little Boy and Fatman made non-stick pans.
Two hundred and fifty thousand
lost in a pair of bright white flashes
meant to make sure
we wouldn't have to scrub so hard.

I tell myself:
duplicity doesn't always imply complicity.

/•/

[16] Are all of our moments, even our most intimate moments, endlessly defined by global concerns?

References Cited in the file of this patent [16]

35

F2 PATENTS

4,173,345 Kelley Anne Couvillion ....March 15, 1976
4,129,710 Andrew Koegel Dillhunt ....August 9, 1975

F1 PATENTS

2,506,482 CX Dillhunt ....…....June 13, 1948
40
2,483,133 Kathleen Mary Koegel ....June 30, 1947
2,427,819 Brian Neff Couvillion ....March 13, 1945
2,415,227 Judith Ebright Couvillion............August 31, 1944

P1 PATENTS

1,956,694 Leola Mary Dillhunt ....March 27, 1923
1,952,088 Mary Jane Koegel ....November 28, 1922
45
1,912,022 Gordon John Koegel ....January 15, 1920
1,887,191 Helen Mauck Ebright ....March 26, 1918
1,849,191 Edwin Dale Ebright ….....…........June 2, 1915
1,827,924 Lawrence Joseph Dillhunt ....October 26, 1913
1,641,339 Arthur Bennett Couvillion .....December 4, 1898
1,634,785 Eugenia Grimillion Couvillion ...…....May, 1898

Within minutes | the nursing staff puts three bands on the newborn | one to match the mother | one to match a person of the mother's choosing | one embedded with a computer chip | to send a signal | to the sensors on the steel doors of the maternity ward || **Most of what we know** | about the migratory patterns of humpback whales | comes from the banding | monitoring and eventual naming | of individual animals || Parents trigger proximity alarms | on their way to the cafeteria | with babe in arms | stand dumbfounded as | shoplifters with ink stains on throwback jerseys || Our retail associates have been explicitly trained to | shadow customers | carrying merchandise into dressing rooms || The doors swing closed | electronic locks snap into position | screens click with anticipation as | the elevator stops dead in its tracks.

Plastic #7 [Nylon]

New York World's Fair, 1939

Her husband envisions the garter:
red, white, and blue,
hand-stitched peek-a-boo eyelets.

Adorned with cellophane bows
and semi-precious Lucite jewels,
The Lady of Chemistry smiles and waves,

swishes the hem of her rayon skirt

then clicks the Pyralin heels
of her patent leather shoes.

Milwaukee, Wisconsin, 1943

Hoping to put a dent
in the roughly 4,000 pairs it takes
to dress the landing gear of a B-29,

Bridgette donates all but one
of the fourteen pairs of nylon hose
from the top drawer of her dresser.

She rolls that remaining pair

into a careful ball, then pushes it
into the back corner of the oak drawer.

She imagines the bombardier
in his dress best:
ballistic nylon flak jacket
cinched tight at the sides

nylon socks

and rot-proof nylon shoelaces,
a twice-packed nylon parachute
within arm's reach.

She worries him to sleep
on his nylon hammock, shrouded
in nylon mosquito netting

inside a nylon tent.

In the solitude of her master bath
after a full day drilling submarine torpedo tubes
at the machine shop on the south side

she paints her legs with pancake makeup
draws a charcoal seam
up the backs of her legs with an eyebrow pencil,

and with a toothbrush, she brushes her teeth.

Wisconsin Avenue, Milwaukee, 1945

Eight days after Japan's surrender,

nylon stockings went back into production.
Bridgette was fourth in line at Gimbels

the day they went on sale.

Osseo, Wisconsin, 1969

From the rust colored couch in her living room
with her bare feet planted in the Berber carpet,
Bridgette watches the astronauts, two of them

squeeze through the open hatch of the LEM.
She watches the war
during the commercial breaks. She watches

the pair plant an unwavering nylon flag
in the dusty soil. The phone rings.

Herselves

Epistolary is a premise
with distributive properties:

to conceive of
speciation is specious:

a mail carrier, only
the penultimate metaphor:

a poet is not at all / surprised by science

/•/

placing a piece of what
once was Henrietta,

a mother of five alive and well
[here I am, the tourist

staking my claim]
in the kingdom

of "animalia," suddenly now

amongst the likes of
(algae, amoebae and euglena)

/•/

A cell's internal
workings, involutions and

volume's squabble
with surface area

has many mouths / and mine
is a cacophony of one

/•/

Numerology

seven

On the way back to the apartment
I stop for detergent.
Aluminum cakes my body
clings to every hair.

The landlady asked me again last night
to scrub the stain of grey dust
from the porcelain of the bathtub.

Leaf is All

The firefly on the burdock
                               too much light
in early morning to
say function.

Being non-reason is
reason enough.
My father hedges down

the prairie path
    my own knees creak
today, my thirty-eighth birthday.

As good a day as any to notice
that anything tends to mean
        something

in the gap between *before*
and *after*

Yet is this the splendor but the heralding

We are walking around a smallish
sink in the prairie. The right word?

Clinging to the moment, the grass
says nothing. I have said everything
meaning to be a good person.

I've done the math.
Think about me doing the math,
he says

        never dark enough
for metaphor, really

In careful number or in wild profusion

all cup plants, all burdock
all purple cone flowers, all quaking
aspen.

NOTES

Leaf is All
The italicized lines are taken from Goethe's poem "The Metamorphosis of Plants," trans. Heinz Norden (except where they aren't).

Notes on Numerology
18   The italicized lines are taken from the poem "Some Trees" by John Ashbery.

A horse, a woman, and a man
The line "How high is have?" is taken from Theodore Roethke's poem "Where Knock is Open Wide."

Herselves
Henrietta Lacks was born in Roanoke, Virginia, on August 1, 1920. At the age of four, following the death of her mother, she moved to Clover, Virginia, to live with her paternal grandfather and work on the family's tobacco farm. In 1942, Henrietta and her husband Day relocated, with their two eldest children, to Turner Station, Maryland, where wartime demand for steel was creating jobs. In 1951, following an exam in the public ward at Johns Hopkins Hospital, Henrietta's cervical tumor cells were used without her knowledge to establish HeLa, the first immortal human cell line.

A detailed account of Henrietta Lacks and the HeLa cell line can be found in the books *The Immortal Life of Henrietta Lacks* by Rebecca Skloot (from which the details above were drawn) and *A Conspiracy of Cells* by Michael Gold.

30   The image of the Ferris wheel is taken from Rebecca Skloot's account of Henrietta Lacks sharing her cancer diagnosis with her cousins.

30   Alexis Carrel was a Franco-American surgeon who, in collaboration with his assistant Montrose Burrows, coined the term "tissue culture" and then formally defined it in 1911.

During the second decade of the twentieth century, the pair worked to establish the possibility of an immortal biological object, separate from the body. Carrel and Burrows settled on a visually impressive culture of embryonic chicken heart cells, which continued to "beat" in rhythmic pulse, even after being isolated from the original tissue fragment. This tissue culture eventually became widely known to the public as "the immortal chicken heart." In the 1960s, experiments definitively established the limited lifespan of normal, non-cancerous cells, like those in Carrell's chicken heart culture.

An account of Carrel and the immortal chicken heart can be found in *Culturing Life: How Cells Became Technologies* by Hannah Landecker.

44 The italicized lines are taken from L. Van Valen, "HeLa, a new microbial species," *Evolutionary Theory*, 10(2): 1991.

89 The line "A poet is not at all surprised by science" is taken from Zukofsky's *A-12*.

    The italicized lines are taken from L. Weasel, "Feminist Intersections in Science: Race, Gender and Sexuality Through the Microscope," *Hypatia*, 19(1): 2004.

3,068,518

The original patent language for "Apparatus for Molding Hollow Plastic Products" was retrieved from *Free Patents Online* (http://www.freepatentsonline.com/3068518.html).

38 The three equations in footnote two are those used to calculate biorhythms. The concept of biorhythms was introduced by German physician and numerologist, Wilhelm Fliess, who—after discovering he could represent any number in relation to the numbers 23, 28, or both—concluded the human body must be inherently governed by combinations of 23- and 28-day periods.

38 Type I statistical error, or an error of the first kind, is equivalent to a false positive. This kind of error is committed when a researcher mistakenly rejects the null hypothesis (that there will be no effect), and, as a result, accepts the experimental hypothesis that there *is* an effect.

20 & 84 World population estimates from 1890 to 2000 were retrieved from the *History Database of the Global Environment* compiled by the PBL Netherlands Environmental Agency (http://themasites. pbl.nl/tridion/en/themasites/hyde).

    Population estimate for the year 2010 as well as half-decadal growth rate coefficients for the years 1950-2000, were retrieved from the United Nations, Department of Economic and Social Affairs, Population Division (http://esa.un.org/wpp/unpp/panel_population.htm).

    My friend, statistician Chris Shuck, generated the global population estimates embedded in the text of the patent (replacing the original patent numbers). I've included his astonishingly poetic methodology in his own words for interested readers:

Population growth typically follows an exponential model. That was assumed to be true. It was also assumed that global population estimates before World War II were highly variable—and that from 1950 on they were much more accurate.

For pre-1950 estimates, a natural log transform of the population estimates was used. This is typically used when trying to linearize population growth data. The transformed data showed three distinct linear growth periods: 1890 to 1920 (A), 1930 to 1950 (B), and 1970 to 1990 (C). The decade of 1960—commonly known as the baby boom decade—was thrown out as an outlier.

For each growth period, yearly population estimates were calculated using the transformed line fit. For each birthday in this time span, the untransformed yearly global population estimates sandwiching the birthday were taken. A constant day-to-day growth coefficient was then calculated to get the birthdate estimate.

For post-1950 estimates, the estimates were considered correct—not estimates (model C above was abandoned, given the higher accuracy of the post-1950 numbers). The United Nations half-decadal growth estimates were leveraged, which suggest that growth rates in the first half of the decade are different than the second half of the decade.

For birthday estimates in these years, this information was incorporated to calculate annual population estimates. For a given birthdate, the sandwiching year estimates were identified and daily estimates were calculated given a constant growth coefficient.

Plastic #7 [Nylon]

86   This poem is indebted to the scholarship of Jeffrey L. Meikle, and his book *American Plastic: A Cultural History*: "Although not exactly a plastic, at least not when used as a fiber, nylon offered an almost pure case study of the domestication process to which Americans submitted plastic after the war was won."

About the Author

Drew Dillhunt is the author of the chapbook *3,068,518* (Mudlark, No. 39, 2010). His writing has appeared in *VOLT*, *Eclectica*, *Tarpaulin Sky*, and *Jacket* and as well as anthologies from both Leaf Press and Shabda Press. An early version of *Leaf Is All* was a finalist for the National Poetry Series. He's released two albums of songs, including one with the band Fighting Shy, and is currently a member of the Seattle-based band Answering Machines. He lives in the Beacon Hill neighborhood of Seattle, where he serves as Associate Editor of Hummingbird Press.

www.ingramcontent.com/pod-product-compliance
Lightning Source LLC
Chambersburg PA
CBHW080546090426
42734CB00016B/3218